Annmarie O'Connell

GLOCK

Annmarie O'Connell's **Glock** is savage and street-wise, delineating a world punctured by addiction, poverty and intimate violence, in a voice that cuts to the truth of human experience like a switchblade. These poems are urgent, necessary, and ferociously oracular, with moments of unlikely grace punching through like a "fist among stars." I won't soon forget them.

> — **Paula McLain**
> author of *The Paris Wife*
> and *When the Stars Go Dark*

This is a book where you will see grief and light, and know that there are "fistfuls of loss," and there are "dirt beds," but in the end you will find hope because "this morning's light / gives you a certain gentleness / over the long slope of your nose." The lyric tilt of these poems is no easy thing to achieve. They are daring, they sparkle, blaze, and they remind us that "a shaft of sunlight enters the earth / the way death enters us / so miraculously inside." The knowledge such miracles is in itself a miracle, found in grief. How to go on with it? Why? Because, perhaps, as the author admits, "the baby's asleep beside me." These are beautiful, revealing poems.

> — **Ilya Kaminsky**
> author of *Deaf Republic*
> and *Dancing in Odessa*

Annmarie O'Connell

GLOCK

Pierian Springs Press

Library of Congress Control Number: 2022933851
ISBN 978-1-953136-13-8

1st edition, paperback
Type set in Adobe Jenson Pro, licensed from Adobe
Art by Grandfailure, licensed from Adobe
Cover Design by Kurt Lovelace

PierianSpringsPress.Com
Sheridan, Wyoming

*"If I feel physically as if the top of my head were taken off,
I know that is poetry."*

Emily Dickinson

I

II

———◆·◆———

I

My sister finally swallowed her anti-psychotic meds

at the exact same time
Jesus flowered in her
the doctor said He would

show us our awful
every time she says God's name
every religious text
we squirm

The Lord Himself Goes Before You
When You Dine With The Lord
You Never Go Hungry

Jesus floods my throat
even in this packed church
kneeling elbow to elbow

my sister's grace falls
out of my side wound
& stupid me

I never even knew
I was butchered
until the bloody fork
landed on my merciful
life

Mom's Risperidone

is killing her. I sing this to you once:
killing her. She is
the bowl of a spoon dripping
tobacco and trailer park,
a roar of diesels
runs over her breastbone.
All the mountains
in my life
are fists of my mother.
I do not waste one drop
when I see her voice taken
out of her body and put
in a stunted star
that always moves
away from me
in a night that twiddles my hair
by the root no matter
where I go. I braid a trail
in the dirty south side
street. This is a daughter
carving a path off to God
then kicked to her knees-a psalm
hung from her big mouth.
Flag her in
from the dark. Tell her
where to go.

Under every skirt is a slip

under mine, he tells me,
is a life of them
when we drive
right through Belvidere into the trailer park.
All the other railroaders fast asleep.
I am trying to stay
sober in this trailer with my AA sponsor.
He was born
twenty-six years before me
on a table just like this.
When he finally convinces me
to have sex
I say my own name
like my very first word: *Annie.*
I am just some girl dumb,
almost despicable
on his nerves
but he knows I should be dead
so he gets up
as if he really loves me
to peel the potatoes.

This is not hell you are swimming in baby

it's my womb
this is our side street
you got a hold of my demons
in there a surge of lilac in something already dying
baby you are the skull of your mother
holding on fast and guess what you might live yet
you might be in one piece or be free too much
alone in your pain you still fly like a boat
be the resistance
you're so beautiful you break my eyes
once you were a feather
now you crash in on America breathing heavy into a sheer blouse
I pray your heart stays in one piece
my heart is hurling stones at whatever hunts you
we move to each other steps
constantly blooming

I am sorry for not helping

you burn down
the heroin house after your white, cold
wounds woke up in their clothes.
People like us do something
in your wool jacket
split right in half,
like the foreman's lip my mother busted
in at the factory after he called her out of her name.
We didn't eat
Tell me about how you sleep now & get to dream
of your dead brother then wake up
still with his body
stuffed in the corner.
Held up to light,
he is a letter you get to read.
Thanks for saying that, *light*
Your life is the sound of glass
ruining us like when loves feet are too far away.
When the person you love
loses everything
he is some strange ghost
& I did nothing for once
except speak out
welcome home

Before the break-up of our country

I get lost so they say stay
where you are. Every day of the year
I want to be found. Imagine ourselves
meeting each other. Imagine hot sunlight and stepping out
    to the sound of mockery,
this baffling country cracking my radiant sister as she turns
    to share a vision
with me. We sneak back into sadness like the lover
mumbling and arriving into your heart. She is asking
to be a wolf. She is really a tiny fire for a vacant
room. Sit down quietly before the others arrive.
This town is a long bench of sleep. All the houses hang
their silver and hope to be awakened. No one is looking
at the axe. Let me hold you for once,
your dirty beard
sobbing its gratitude.

It is 4am

My neighbor
is drunk and yelling outside of my door.
He is screaming
he wants to fuck me. He is breaking bottles
of Old Style and falling into traffic.
I lay in bed listening. He doesn't know
that I already put myself inside him. We are both overbrimming
with nightmares. His sister is dying
of Leukemia. She is this Monday's rain,
a last brief shimmer of life
you forget that is happening
until you walk outside and feel
it beating down on your skin. You get to see her body
falling into loss. Falling into temptation.
This is how you remember
we are alive.
Right now everyone
on this block is drunk.
I am making something of the sea
before it swallows the God
wising up in me. God is always a switchblade
to my throat. I take him by the shoulders tight.
With one pulse of love,
our heartbeat is a single thing.
Change is the biting whip I put my lips to.
I am almost catching up
with me.

I do not take a drink

He strokes my hair awkwardly.
I get blindsided by an everlasting joy.
I wonder if his mother
ran through all the rooms
looking for cigarettes. I wonder if her heart
was so cold the windows shut themselves.
Right now nothing
stirs in me.   I pilot the plane. I wait several
seconds. Right now everything
stirs in me. I pilot the plane. His secret
life throbs in my hand. I do not take
a drink. I find out his other girlfriend is rich.
It's like we live in two other worlds
She says I have a 63rd street
education.   Sometimes she calls me sweetheart.
I have never studied in Hong Kong. I have never left
the country. I wanted to go to Iraq. My dad
said *I will kill you myself.* 63rd street education.
I pilot the plane. Having survived so much
I am fully armed and riding
alone. I put my fist against
something imagined. I wait
several seconds. I do not take a drink. I put my fist
among stars.

Some hours are larger

than others when I reach over
to close my mother's blue robe
sickness swallowing her hard
& I do this all clumsily
with scabs on my knees, thin eyelids
I'm a little terrible
this is all like seeing myself
a junkie
even when my son came out of me
I couldn't stop for good
until the second one
snipped my strings,
a puppet rolling around
in the dusty pile of my life
& now the warmth of their bodies
pull me tighter to some vivid
different sun, some smaller hour
where even the absent arms
of my mother become nothing
but a flicker of water over dinner
my mother
making buckets out of hospital baths
wash rags out of t-shirts
I remember her
washing her hair last in the shower.

My mother is trying to die in the other room

The other room is tiny. Brown furniture lines the walls
so I can barely stand by her bedside. I can barely fit in the room
my mother is trying to die in. I can't afford the car
I am driving. My mother told me I shouldn't
drive because I wasn't God-
saved and I was always sipping on something.
I can't remember or hold on to anything my
mother said
always in circles
You have tragedy in your blood
she told me
I am good at listening in circles.
I can tell you that my mother
gave birth to me and that I was the moon
like really something when I gushed out
of her body without some way to escape my blood,
tiny particles of botched DNA that rumble
through me, beneath my neck,
in the cuffs of my shoulders.
I am waiting to be worn in love
that makes me fall to my knees

before her, dismantled so quickly
I am the parts that she made me.
I am waiting for something to arrive
that never arrives.
I can't even fit in the room
my mother is trying to die
in. My brutal blood
pulsing through my veins,
losing on purpose losing every-
thing.

It's been three years

since I made the case to go free.

The house I lived in was a genuine life desert.

My mother will never know

I recovered from so many secrets.

The hush of a secret making systems,

remaining over water.

My sobriety,

like extreme weather,

my attempt to measure

my life in shades

of blue numbness.

My body,

even your uncle

reminds me

of my body.

I wanted my father to take to the street

with his crusader heart,

find me in my drunken stupor.

Just three years ago

I picked apart a family inside me

when there was not a family inside me.

My mother will never know

that I am more body bag

than fire pit.

That sometimes when I hold my son

I want some other version

of my life happening.

I mean, what is a *mother*

doing inside *me?*

Do not tell my children

I can't remember what it feels

like to not want to wander

into a lake swiftly and

accurately.   I need more black cherry

and citrus   more *mother*

Please do not tell my children

the word *mother*

this half empty closet

a possibility   a poverty

It's not that I'm too good

for the Presidential Suite.

It's just never wise to rush

into things. I wonder if the still life

couple on 56th street rushed into each other

in a quiver of a moment. A violent kick.

He is standing in front of her

in his construction clothes. His boots are honey brown.

He is staring into her eyes like they are little stories.

They are human and breaking

under each other's tongue. They are floating

weightless in their real bodies. If true love

exists, I believe we can take a cab there.

It is almost impossible to get a cab

on the south side. Soon enough

it will be noon.

The face of my mother passes me by

in space for no particular reason.

I can't take it off.

I can't take off her body that deteriorates

slow like a sunflower

in its skinny vase, long yellow-brown

petals fall off one by one
onto the rickety kitchen table.
You count them with your fingers.
You count them
up and amount to everything.

I lie in the road remembering

my friend who took out a Glock

and shot towards the bus unexpectedly.

I still love him

let me hear you say:

I love him.

He is 63rd street,

a little boy heart-starved

for America, cruelty spraying

in its pot.

Who is unknown to cruelty?

Even you in your perfect body

a hidden monster hungry,

you ate no better.

Pushing your tongue

into a promise

in the dark is easy.

I remember running

leaps of nerve

taking off in an attack plane

let me tell you

my eyes welling

with spirit & rifle

what they shout at me
Don't get too smart
as I sharpen instead
of sing.

Five dimes is all I have

for the man begging in the street.
He barely opens his hand
attempting to hide the sores
on his palms with a quick
mention of a storm hovering
over, too heavy to begin
its beating down
on both of us. I tell him
to open up so I can get
a look at them-so
crusted over and deep
like breathing,
that I immediately
start to feel like one is growing
on my body. A little pulse shoots up my arm.
But everything is not about me. It's about
something like my AA sponsor
told me: you can even bring two dogs
in from the rain.

The cracked veins of a green leaf are imperfect

but intentionally touching at exactly the right places
so they become almost beautiful all by themselves
just like in the way that man will never love you.
In your rear-view mirror,
you see a stranger you have to love
because he is sweating in his red bandana and tired from work
and you realize he really isn't a stranger at all.
He catches you staring at his tired eye and now
he's another person who just doesn't like you.
You can't help it if it reminds you of how we scatter
ourselves out into the dark of our lives
begging to come back an ocean.
But there's no ocean here. Just a man standing
in his own kitchen window by the kitchen sink
as you drive down the road.
Suddenly your heart
is the dirtiest dish—you can't forget
the sound it makes
clanging against the other dishes.

I.

when the boys carried my limp body

upstairs to bed   *140 lbs. of dead weight*

they laughed   I couldn't stay straight

& be in the world   a bellyful of burning

II.

here's my chisel.   here's my body   here's my fishing pole here's

something invented to be silenced: the noise of my rape
        in your bare hand

forgive me south side I have outgrown   your colorful fist

III.

the woman at the AA meeting said

you're too pretty for AA/they will murder you

my blood of predators

13th step sponsor   holds me down the motel room

south side sobriety   killed me

IV.

Let me go   love song of my life

my blood of felons   south side you have turned   your backside

your daughter getting choked out again single mother
      & my children's father sells dope

        (the rug being pulled out from under us)

V.

in the church office   the sound of my mother dying
      ripples up the holy water

spun out hands for food, etc.   the white-haired people say

I hope I don't see you again my blood of drunk Grandfather
      shows me his penis

I sit in my crib a volume of celestial terror   *Do you know my kind?*
      Do you?

VI.

The song of my life

playing   too long

VII.

Lucky me: a woman

sweet, too

sugar heart: anger red

When my sister lost her mind

it was a riot flowing electric in my fingers.
My fingers remember suffering.
I was a sail in the cross-
wind, flapping & shaking to the sound
of my sister. I fled this woman
for a few years to track down God.
God was a flick between the thought
and the next thought. She is schizophrenic
jumping out of ambulances
running from government
infested needles. She is so beautiful
it hurts me. Once I saw a man
stumble out of a taxi & into a bar
so carefree, the sight of stone.
I swore my sister was loosening
& swilling inside him like water
by the window we danced as little girls
switching hands, one foot to another.
Love is beautiful like this.
Love is learning
all your life
how to hit
for your sister,
how to fake
the music.

The woman muffled in me

carries her own burdens.
She is the split lip
in a checkout line
Go ahead & look
at her Link Card
her babies
sounding like a rug
being pulled
out from under us.

She opens
the light and is nowhere
inside him. A man is a larger boat.
She is alone on the water.

I am not a Chinese painter
I am not salt
I am not silver or gold
I am not

The sound of my
mother dying
is names of people
you might recognize.
I am in her face
I cannot understand
what she is trying to tell me

finally is *I love you*
finally is the song
of your life playing too long
finally is the word

      rising

the lawyer calls me

to talk about my ex-boyfriend
and *the situation* that occurred
between us
        the situation is called *the situation*
because even to powerful women
there are limits
       on my body
there are limits
       to truth

not today Ms.
not *the situation*
In fact say that

felony domestic battery felony domestic battery felony domestic
   battery with attempted murder

the branches creak and crack a neck
I was born half buried under a tree
go out and play but don't go near your mother
go out and play but don't
I let it begin
The answer is always the same
I let it begin
The limits of my body
saturated in guilt

Ms. lawyer woman says he wants to get his law license
and they are thinking about it
so please tell her about *the situation*
His money expunged the record

Goddamn there is no record
        of my life

It's hard to tell you
money makes me invisible
a tied dog howling
I lost count
of myself Luckily there is this
remembered sadness
my ptsd
(I have lost count of myself)
Keep track of my situation
It is Thanksgiving
My tiny children run around
my drunk body lying face first
on the basement floor
It is Thanksgiving
One week before I enter outpatient
treatment (not law school)
for the second time
after *the situation*

Ms. I am going
to be in high mountains
soon By Christ
go ahead and tell me
about when they sold my life
How did they bargain
        the price

I woke this morning wearing

an old red shirt. I soured myself

all the way to market. People

talk in their important people

voices. They say people things like: *I can see*

through her shirt. Can't you love me

like you did in December? Listen,

I've got the blues every day.

But not the James Booker blues. He had

a dispute with a record contractor. He told

someone Ringo Starr pulled his eye out. Even

after Ringo did it, he said he didn't think

it essential to have support. Now I hear you

say my name. I hear you say it

in the library. I hear you become that man

who almost starts to cry at the back table

because of the bombings. *Three people dead so far.*

He reaches out both of his arms as if to finally fall

into someone and break completely. He wants

me to lie down in the corridor

of his body just so

I can weep beside

him. A house on top

of a house. Or to rejoice

over the possibility.

II

She drank to forget a man

who could not love her
back. So she wasn't fire at all,
but a window you don't dare
shut, even in the middle of winter,
because you know it will never
open again. She can see this.
She can say it to your face
like her husband's name.
Once she ran out of the house
naked and woke up
to her neighbor smudging her eye
make-up in bed
with his licked thumb. She screamed inside
her brain first, like accidentally driving through
a stop sign and getting away with it,
a terror you just have
to come to. She hasn't looked
in the mirror since.

Seven Last Words

First Word: Father forgive them. They know not what they do.

      Welcome to the cradle. Sleep where you're damned
      from the beginning. I'm still finishing
      a test. I assure you. They know what

                 they do

Second Word: Today you will be with me in Paradise.

      But I'm so sick of that. It's sad and slow
      and touches my shoulders when I really
      just want it to lean against me. Today

      you will be with me while I get gas.
      I hate getting gas. Today this is

                 Paradise

Third Word: Dear Woman, Here's your son.

He is a shriek of exquisite power.
A Holy Spirit replacement. God
hovering over water. The little

reason I woke up

from my life

Fourth Word: My God, My God, why have you abandoned me?

Mobile, Alabama Oaks Trailer Park.
A swollen creek floods their bodies. Someone
should rescue them. You are in eternity.

I'm full to capacity. This is our
bodily life. We are drowning

with everything we need

Fifth Word: I'm thirsty.

     A fire burns in me. Seeds of terror.
     I'm exploding with love in an oil
     drum. Like water vibrating in the same
     silence as death. The sound of my hand - I

                will miss it

Sixth Word: It's finished.

     Knee-bent. Ashy, stricken, and then knee-bent.
     The most favorable position among
     leaders everywhere originates

                from me

     We're slugging it out in the dark. They said
     it's easy. If you continuously
     open up on any day, you will be

     finished.

                It's not finished

An afterlife is lived in the body.
You said it's like free-falling from your knees
then back into yourself. He has short, dough

fingers.   Dirty fingers from picking
the bottom of a trash can for your spirit..
I want to start over in my body.

                              Watch me rise

I

We move in and out of tragedy then pick a thin layer off just to see it. In the house we say, that's all the oranges. In late Spring, we all leave Earth on an escalator so he fires four shots through the bathroom door to kill her. Like she was an intruder. He said he loved her in his restless body. The lawyer questions him about the precise screaming. He says, I wish she let me know she was there. No one says never again genocide. Another season of trespassing deaths just hit us like a river of grief.

II

The bodies flame into a wild God. A dark matter God
sitting in South Dakota at the bottom of a goldmine-the
quarter of the universe no one has ever seen. Suspended in
its heart is a world too good for us. Sometimes we see a
brief flash of light from twenty five stories high. We die
without knowing the universe. We never know what it's
made of.

III

She is always inventing a way to believe again. I am always
a bedside with long hands fumbling towards me in the
dark. A video camera running beside the bed. When she is
dead, people in thin layers of different flesh will sprint
across that square like pain illuminated in one blast. When
I am dead, the darkest heart screams over the sound of
your scraping chairs what I am.

IV

A rat mother makes one thousand babies in a year then forges them out into the landscape armed with skills. They win or lose or die. My body is a time machine. When it's turned on I am a rat baby without a rat mother holding herself in the dark.

V

This has been going on for God knows how long. Time is shifting away in a house plant. Time is shifting away in a stack of men. Ask them what they did with time. Ask them why I rethread a needle over and over with a flashlight even though the lights work all my life.

VI

I just woke up again. This room is so small it's a dime. I
wish I knew how to scream perfectly. Once I met a girl
named Eleanor. I'm not like her. She is nothing like me.
She is not into forever horror stories. She is a turtle with a
beautiful face and wonderful eyelids and specialized
lighting. She dances into a green box and comes out
Eleanor.

VII

If you leave the knife on the table, I'll let you bite my lip
until the blood runs down my chin. Stop looking up when
you throw me against the bricks. Let me slide my hands
through gravel as you step over my body. I lock you up then
wait like a welt. When you get out and in the backseat,
you're as filthy as a bed with your hands trembling for a fix.
Around my neck they still craving things. If I'm on top, I
think about what living people do. If I'm on bottom, I can
feel my mouth almost ask you to build me a free woman.

VIII

People squirm at the living room inside me where a young
girl hangs on invisible hinges. No one believes that wildfire
below burning the pink-white flowers off her party dress.
You have to squint just to see her little thigh blister open
like a bird that still sings minutes before the blade enters
its gut. Her smoldering ash — the only reliable witness to
my life.

IX

The five o'clock shadow wears white overalls and nervously
smiles toward me in the crowded grocery store. His cart
full of delicate cookies and bright red fruit. He doesn't
know that I have already left this moment, even when it is
happening, I am as anonymous as the smooth purple city,
the brown hat squeezing the small head of a boy.
Everything up to now is a secret with teeth and bones
trying to climb onto an old table just to pull the switch on
my body, to light it up like a yellow leaf.

X

After something like a dream, look out your window to the
left of the curb for a tiny quarter stain that the streetlight
always makes flicker like a blue-gray sky dragging its long
face right before the next rain. Or what God throws at you
from the heights — just enough to prove it was there.

I read about Community Violence Exposure

in urban youth
& the negative psychological outcomes
depression, generalized anxiety, post-traumatic stress disorder
(piles of metal looming like overgrown company)
And here I am
triggered away again.
I call it *booming backward.*
I remember my dear body
getting beat down in the street,
my teenage mouth
against slabs of Chicago concrete.
As she kicked my head,
I left my childhood
in yellow orbs of streetlight.
My cracked voice closing under the
palm of a girl. You can say I felt
embarrassed that I was too drunk
to get up. I stammered often
as a street girl.
This is how it goes:
grief in a paper bag
distorting the trajectory of my whole life.
Am I fit for love? I'd never knew it existed
outside or inside my wicked self,
or at the counter of my mother
her matted hair, that wild flicker of red
guiding me for too long.

My landlady removes laundry

from the line right before

a downpour. It's so lovely

to watch her win, even a little.

Certain nights Pawel is drunk

and passes out by her door.

Everything is easier in dreams

for honest people. I wake up in the morning

a little rough silhouette starving

for the same particle and wave: light.

I leave out a plate of bacon

then step over his body. I touch him

once just to make sure there is no secret

hope inside what is decaying this ship,

collapsing it right

on the spot.

The bed sheets are smeared

with shards of bone
from the dog gnawing at 3AM.
The pit of your stomach
deep in the core of your heart
is a thousand people living without seeing
themselves. Every one of them
like a blow to your head
with a tire iron
making you ashamed
of the thick light
between your teeth.
I must have loved you
days and nights before you rattled
in my life, stumbling over
a small river of lions. The brain
inside you blossoming
in my body like the music
of a dirty bus station
where the people strum
then calm us
to the brink.

The hurricane   in the middle

of your life starts
like that wretched idea   you lean over
                                 put in my head

it happens that   during the hurricane
you're crammed with nothing   you need
even the floor of the world   even the furniture

everything   *staying*

after
you're never   magnificent

            you gleam
            you leap
            you hold

up my street
that sluggish figure again   entering my bed-
room   a shadow coming
into snow

don't make me
put your funeral tie   on the dresser
don't make me
cry out to you   from the hospital bed
flicker your eyebrows   *the day my brain stops working*
take me to some place on 63rd street   touch my face on 63rd street
wrap your fingers   around my wrist on 63rd street

home is a gasp   a plane suffocating
in the clouds   hear my heart
demand a life

My mother is so poor

she cannot love me.
When we look at the one photograph
of her pregnant belly, my tiny body inside
her like a poisoned flower,
she tells me: *I wanted to end it*
All my life I've been a ghost
through the screen door
whipping my horse
across the finish line.

My mother is so poor
she rode a bus
through the Back of the Yards
all night with her sisters
& brothers until her felon father sobered up
to maybe take a break from beating
all of them with a hammer.
Other days she slept
in a laundromat on 31st street
so he wouldn't come
into her bed with his empty eyes.

When he touched my own body
I thought *I'm simply part of the damned*
no one save me
but then the need grew for stars,
echoes of lilac, so now I tilt my head
to at least look at her
(illness destroying her insides)
& I shake down a dream
where we disappear outback
by the low hanging branches.
In my dream she holds

her arms out & I run to her
needy & luckless.
The whole damn universe
weighing me down
when I let her squeeze me
for the very first time
it's still.
Please don't go.

Everyone is a reflection

       in a pool   saying my name

       my name my name

       I want to run towards them

to put my face to their faces

this is me and I will twitch to death in this very same body

I have already started drowning

       in your hair smells of chlorine

so you are finally familiar when you teach

my body how to sing clean

       la-la-la-la-la la

not dirty screaming

everything doesn't have to be a memory

my brain smudged up   against glass in the motel room

 so you can   get a good look at what will push me

       off the cliff

my dna unravels   a lighting bolt

       off the cliff

disrupting the neurotransmitter party

       off the cliff

no lights

I experience pleasure

for now

no lights

I remember my name

for now

Everyone is saying it

for now

Everyone is talking

the most beautiful sound in the world

for now

Don't tell me to remember beauty

I am a DNA disaster

I am a relic of time counting down

your city is afraid

of my urgency

I want your eyes to fill with all the people

learning how to rise to the surface

I want to swallow all of you

       Come over me

Come misplace   your animal

over me

a hero-turning

Visiting Grandpa in Pontiac State Prison

I spy   a run down Buick

my working-class   hand me down shoes

Venture sweatpants   smoke from Mom's Winston circling

her pregnant belly   we never read

the newspaper articles   what he did to other children

They say I'm still lucky

     I spy my mother   hug his prison blues

     (please remember their brains are not working)

     I spy trailer park teeth

     I spy a smile   my mother makes me   half dead floating

     Don't touch me   *don't put my fire out*

     I spy   a mouth   everything doesn't have to be

     a memory

     I spy

     his mouth   every mouth I see moving

     in the tight black street

Drunk & Huntington's

diseased   I barely dress myself

in a white t-shirt   I beat

my chest   my grandfather

the prison yard   Both of our brains

already stop growing   slow and quiet nerve

cells cells cells

nothing is working   my brain will

        stop working

somebody has to love me

I lay down   an orphan

Look at my assassin's face I stopped asking

        for the lighthouse

The city isn't a skyline

"Chicago ain't nothin' but a blues band."
Sunnyland Slim

That's pretend.

If you're lucky, the city is your Mama

chasing down the freight train rolling

over your body. If not,

it's Loretta in the back-

room piano West side soul

Magic Sam calls it music to strip.

Call it Gentlemen Jim's and The Pit.

Loretta really wants to get out

of the animal city. She is a half price

booty dilemma you can't ignore. Weigh it

into the performance,

her thin alligator face doin' it right

now. The men tell her

they summer in Cambridge

and France with five hundred cameras,

with saxophones and trumpets

they don't know

how to use.

Loretta is an independent scholar

with novel theories on Hot Jazz

and Fist Wars. When she dies

no one claims her. Her body sits in

county morgue then goes

unmarked in a wooden box.

Loretta is thousands

of nameless bodies speaking one

central heart beating

deep down in the vicious

city dirt.

I had my first paid job

at 12 years old, a groundskeeper
for the local little league field,
every time the south side drunk
in charge wobbled over to scream at me

about being a girl on the baseball team,
about picking up enough trash with the pointed
stick, I saw his 9-year-old son's name imprinted
on the giant orange and black sign
hanging behind his bald head.

He lost him so quickly on one of those frigid
fall mornings in September,
back when he used to walk upright
and be a little soft, sometimes holding his son
by the back of the neck and smiling
into the rear view,
and sometimes not.

I am a knot tied

to the root of you

unbound only by your teeth
Woody Guthrie sings, *it is none of their business how you treat me*

His brain stopped working

still

love-struck
Hand-cuffed to forearm

tremor dancing tremor dancing
garden box from spine
to heavy feet

still

I write you under

a tree. Otherwise, you're spoken
automatically: *hello,* big heart. Rattle in your cage.

Let the world gas you
& drip diesel on your tongue

such harshness
tricked out of myself

love is the thing

that wakes me

Acknowledgements

I would like to thank the following publications for which these poems have appeared or are forthcoming:

"Under every skirt is a slip" and "Some hours are larger" are in *Beloit Poetry Journal*

"I" in Section I and "When my sister lost her mind" are forthcoming in *Poetry City, USA*

"the lawyer calls me" appeared in *Rogue Agent*

"I woke this morning wearing" appeared in *Sixth Finch.*

"This is not hell you are swimming in baby" and "I lie in the road remembering" is forthcoming in *Thoughtcrime Press/Not My President* Anthology

'I do not take a drink", 'My mother is trying to die in the other room" appeared in *Room Magazine*

"It's been three years" appeared in *Juked*

"The cracked veins of a green leaf are imperfect" appeared in *Painted Bride Quarterly*

"I, II, III, IV, V, VI, VII, VIII, IX, X, Seven Last Words, The City isn't a skyline" appeared in a chapbook called *Eleanor* published by dancing girl press

"Everyone is a reflection, , Drunk and Huntington's, Visiting Grandpa in Pontiac State Prison, Five Dimes is all I have, The hurricane in the middle," is in the chapbook *hello,* with *Yellow Flag Press*

Annmarie O'Connell

Annmarie O'Connell

Annmarie is a lifelong resident of the south side of Chicago. She is a graduate of New England College's MFA program in Henniker, New Hampshire. Her work has appeared in *Beloit Poetry Journal*, *Sixth Finch*, *Juked*, *Room Magazine*, *Verse Daily*, *Slipstream*, *SOFTBLOW*, *Vinyl Poetry*, *Thrush*, *Escape Into Life*, *2River View* and many other wonderful journals.

Her first chapbook *Her Last Cup of Light* was published by Aldrich Press in 2013. Her first full-length collection of poems, *Your Immaculate Heart*, was released with Trio House Press in 2016. Her fifth chapbook *63rd Street Devotional* was published with Voice Lux in 2017.

GLOCK is her second, full-length work.